MASTER

DIALOGUES *of* LOVE

O MASTER

RACHNA CHOPRA

Ra Publishing

O MASTER
Copyright © 2020, 2002 Rachna Chopra

RA PUBLISHING
Second edition, 2020

ISBN 978-81-901490-0-6

Ra Publishing
848 N Rainbow Blvd #711
Las Vegas, NV 89107

Author contact:
rachna@rachnachopra.com

Cover and book design:
The Book Designers

Dedicated to His Holiness Sri Ganapathi Sachchidananda of Avadhoota Datta Peetham, on occasion of his 60th birth anniversary in Mysore, India, 2002. This revised edition includes poems presented in 2013 at Jesus Datta Retreat Center, Pittsburgh, PA.

CONTENTS

INTRODUCTION

Who is a master? One your heart accepts and your soul recognizes. The moment of meeting him becomes an unforgettable moment in your life, when you feel an unexplained familiarity, and a sense of belonging unsubstantiated by experience. From here on, life charts a whole new course.

The bond between a master and disciple is most intimate. It is firstly and lastly that of pure love. This love is beyond logic, cause, convention or description. No matter how much we try, we cannot fathom the origin of this one link, till we give up trying to understand!

The master is our doorway to experience the unfathomable reality. Like the moon, he passes to us the comforting rays of blazing sun. He becomes the road between our stray and our destination. Fully aware that as we near the source, our hand will leave his, yet works laboriously to dispel our darkness (Gu) with his light (Ru).

When the master enters your life, stand not as an obstruction. Do not auction this one treasure once you have found it. Do not give up this recluse even in exchange of heavens. Do not leave this hard till this beauty begins to reflect in your eyes, and this compassions finds home in your heart.

Where does one find the master? It is the master who finds the disciple, not disciple the master. The real teacher is our own Self, that lives in the rise and fall of our breath. Yet, till such time we realize this unity, ascended masters adorn different masks, and meet us in different lifetimes.

Sometimes the master appears in the king of guises—human! With the same features such as ours, only endlessly more beautiful. This miracle occurs when a realized soul willingly comes down on Earth to be one of us, suffer like us and die like us. Just to steer us home.

To encounter the master in a human form is a benediction indeed. To recognize and follow him, yet greater, because when the mind weaves its web, we begin to doubt. Ignorance swells, confusions mount. Hence, to be able to surpass doubt and follow is the greatest blessing of all.

The overwhelming wave of emotion for one's spiritual friend acquires many hues, but words prove insufficient to express the longing to become one with this wholeness. This intense devotion tills the hearts soil, and prepares it to receive the gift of awakening.

Here, the dialogue begins of your words with the great silence. You venture to find out whence is this miracle erupting. Enquiry begins, search for the way back home. Unimagined horizons open up. You begin to fade. There is a rising, an explosion, a union shall we say, when one is everywhere and nowhere at once. A cry of bliss pierces the heart, and in a language other than words you exclaim—O master!

PROLOGUE

While I sleep, you keep awake,
as only a wakeful one
can awaken slumbering souls.
While I wander, you wait.
Or else we both shall get lost on the way.
While I eat, you starve.
For I eat for two or often more than two.
While I weep and while I scroll in laughter,
you keep still, to absorb the sound I create.
Like the silence after applause.
While I accomplish and achieve,
you stay stationed in non-doing
to soak in the mess I make.

When I call for you with passion,
you smile with dispassion.
For you are none other than my master.
You dispel my darkness
with your light.

Precisely the reason why
what is for me a task,
is for you play.
What is for me love,
is for you compassion.
For me what is remorse,
for you 'tis bliss.

Passage of time that pains me,
ruffles you not.
Ghastly errors that blemish me,
taint you not.
Neither are your limbs adorned with ornaments,
as your senses are calm and rested.
Unlike mine
that need anklets and rings,
so their unrest may not show.

Isn't a single unstitched cloth
all you require
to cover your frame?
That too of one color, ochre.
With a lone embellishment, you.
Perfumed with just one fragrance, yours.
A pair of wooden sandals all your feet ever graced,
while they walked to a million destinations.
A staff of truth, all that stood by your side.

Quizzical indeed are you.
Your beautiful eyes are forever open.
Unlike mine
that are sleepy with wine or ignorance.
Yet you do not see, nor point out my follies.
Your feet are unchained.
Still you do not rush to tend to me,
when I wound myself.

When I have forgotten you,
you emerge from nowhere
and attract attention.
When I get enticed by your beauty,
you move away.
When I ask from you a favor,
you exhibit denial.
When I have in me no more desire left,
my lap overflows with abundant fruit.
You indeed are strange.

Yet I know
that your house is the only I can knock,
when the world shows me the door.
When I speak you listen with care.
Tell me—what draws a heavenly being such as you
to an earthling like me?
Why do you walk barefoot on my porch
in scorching heat,
where previous night I shed tears?

You indeed are my only true relation,
my sole link from whence I came.
For you know the way back.
For you never moved.
While I ran hither and thither,
and fruitlessly so.

Call it my faith in you,
or call it conviction in my love for you,
no matter how imperfect.
I have the boldness to embrace you,
and touch your face with bare hands,
dirty with a thousand sin.

I hold the intent of bringing you flowers,
whose fragrance melts with one whiff
of a whimsical breeze.
Whose beauty
takes no longer than a day to droop.
And offer them at your altar
that perfumes for eternity.
And glows at all seasons
by reflection of your blinkless beauty.

I have the courage
to shun this illusion cast upon me,
and run to you.
Do you have the audacity to accept?

I have the eye to recognize you
amongst a million faces,
hear your whispers in this deafening noise.
Without a secret code between the two of us,
I can tell in the thick of night,
that the knock at my heart
is none other than yours.
Whereas your recognizing me
is not such a task.
Considering for you,
there are no two faces
nor a noise!

I am ready to relinquish
a world that may be for you unreal,
but for me is still true.
Do you have the courage
to set aside your asceticism,
and embrace me?

Do you tremble on my advent
as I, when I glimpse you depart
from my dream at crack of dawn?

Do you know
since the time you left,
the music has not changed
and it is still night.
The sun has now decided
to shine only on you.

If I yearn to see you,
you too must be waiting
behind your sober demeanor, I know.

After all,
the wait must end
like everything else.

PRAYER

He walks as if he knows. He smiles. Now he stops. Now he moves. The master of all arts, all hearts.

Accept me, the little flame.
O great fire!

Where music is, you are. Where fragrance is, you are. Where beauty is, you are. Where peace is, you are. Where truth is, you are. Where love is, you are. Where light is, you are. Where yoga is, you are. Where bhakti is, you are. Where shakti is, you are. You are everywhere, O master. But to my heart, you are very near!

When you are the goal,
just the journey is important.

You are neither a dream, a wish nor a prayer. You are neither the heart nor the mind, aye, not even the soul. You are neither here, nor there, nor this nor that. You are never his, hers or theirs. You cannot be loved (enough), hated or ignored. You are an untouched contact, an unspoken message, an uncorded relation. You are an ungraspable emotion, an unsolved mystery. You are a vibration that eludes the mind but stirs the heart. You are the voice of my silence, the yearning of my soul.

You reveal everything by the way you walk, speak, look. Only we do not have eyes to see, nor ears to hear, that your footstep is lighter than a feather fall. Your sight, more fulfilling than a full moon night. Your gait, more enchanting than that of a deer. Your gaze, more enveloping than the rising ocean wave. Your presence, subtler than the subtlest. Your love, more uplifting than any other.

You were seated in front like an emperor in his zone. Blessing people who queued to touch your throne. I mingled with the crowd but could not courage to go close. So you turned into a flower that I could touch and behold!

You are a lotus, a divine being. Who with ordinary eyes cannot be seen. This point is missed by a mundane mind that you are a rare find. A heart encased in daily chores finds it hard to believe, that here is a space that has no doors, or a form that has sheen. That you are a lotus, a divine being.

*I glimpse you in the first rays of sun
kissing the earth, in the rise of the
serpent's hood, in the tremble of a flower.
I sight you in a peacock with open wings,
in a woman awaking fresh from sleep, in
a leaf turning yellow. I touch you in the
raindrop curling under my window frame.
Aye, I need not go far. I hear you in the
rise and fall of my own breath.*

Like Nandi facing her Shiva, I freeze in the posture of staring at you. Spellbound, mesmerized…beholding you.

Where mind ends, you begin. When silence begs to speak, you are near. When from an experience of pain arises bliss, you are close. You are witness to my love, my diversion from love, to my bondage and urge for freedom. You are there, whether I see you or I don't, whether I trust you or I don't. You were here when I was born, and would hear my last sigh. You can defy my sight, but not my soul.

Wherever you take me, I am ready to follow. My steps are your footprints. My direction is your perfume. My strength is your voice beckoning me. My goal is you. My tears are your separation. My joy is your smile. My penance is yearning to see you. My sacrifice…being away. My desire is to merge in you, but my hope is one single glance! My calm is the unrest for you. My freedom is in bondage to you. My rosary is thoughts of you. My meditation… looking at you. My religion is service to you. Your worship is my karma!

In asking of thee, I have no shame.
In taking from thee, I have none. For you
are my father in heaven, and on earth.
You are my family.

LOVE

When you leave, I sit still. To be touched
by the breeze that brushed past you.

*What the first drop of rain is to the fields,
first ray of sunlight to life on earth, first
stirring in the womb to the mother,
you are to me.*

Make me your echo, so that I may voice what you say, linger when you leave. Make me your echo, your reflection, your bliss, your compassion. Or anything that is inseparable.

31

Take me with you wherever you go.
Wherever you go, keep me with you,
with you always.

*Though I know your blessings are on all
equally, all in your eyes are the same,
I like to think you love me more.*

You hid behind ochre robes, words of detachment, calm pretense and a cool ignore. Yet, I caught a glimpse of your relentless love, though only of the soul! You touched me not, nor let your slender fingers through my hair pace. Yet I returned with a satisfaction, like I received my long due embrace. The final evidence emerged with the parting glance of us two, that revealed clearly that you were more sad to leave me than I was to leave you. I will not tell the world this secret, break not your game. But between us O master, can I give you a name?

*Reveal yourself to me, so that
I may describe you to others.*

Call me the dream sleeping at thy feet,
the wish waiting on that eyelash.
Call me the breeze meeting thy cheek.
The heart clutching at thy robe or the
garland hugging thy seat.
But don't give me a name!

You are silence.
Words cannot describe you.

*As kingdom encircles the king, and stars
the moon, we gather to feast upon you.*

A twitch, a tremble, a sigh.
Few silent offerings before I die.

O master sculptor,
when you finish chiseling me,
will I look somewhat like you?

You are everyone's. I am no one's. You are everywhere. I am nowhere. You are whole. I am full of gaps. You are the Sun. I, not even a ray. I am the beggar. You the chooser. You are the king. Me, a tramp. You are the shimmering summer rain. Me, the parched soil thirsting to engulf you in my fold. You will shower, I know, and mingle in my muddy puddle thoughtless of my color and dirt. But I beseech you still from my miserable plight, 'do not pour! I can offer thee nothing but dearth.'

*How many times shall
I err and apologize?
Kill this mind once and for all, master!*

Each breath is borrowed, each moment is a loan. Each day that I spend is not mine. Even I am yours.

What you are to me, none shall know. You are my blood, my breath, my blessing. My destination as far as eyes can go. What have I done to deserve you? Seeds of this benediction I surely did not sow.

O world, hinder not when
I am moving towards my beloved.
It's a slight I can carry, but a cross
you would wish not to bear.

To every why, there is an answer. But there is no answer to the why I love you. Behind every effect, there is a cause. But there is no cause to the effect 'I love you.' For every quest, there is a quench. But there is no quench for the thirst 'I love you.'

Your love for me seems so great
as compared to my love for you,
that sometimes I feel ashamed
to love thee.

*I draw life's meaning from the
well of your eyes, experience of bliss
from your smile. And my soul's rest
with you seated by my side.*

I go away from you. You pull me back.
What is this bond between us that
I hear your voice in my heart?
Why so much love for me, that
no matter what I do you leave me not.
Wherever I go, you follow me. Why every
wish of mine you fulfill, master?

Cut reveals blood. Cry reveals pain.
You reveal me.

I am not afraid to pass through gates of hell. But how will your feet bear the pain?

There were those that pledged land, and built houses of worship. There were those that toiled lifetimes in your service, and those that offered you their voices, and their vices. But I only trembled at your altar, and decked the dew that fell from my eyes, in words.

Your return, like sword back in sash.
Owner of house in home.
King back on throne.

It is better to be imprisoned in the lock of your gaze than be set free without you. The world will not understand the permanence of this passing moment!

In the kingdom of the beloved,
love is the (only) protocol.

LONGING

*Why don't you accept me, having made
me unfit for everyone else?*

At moments of departure, you cajole me,
calm me, mould me, sway me. So that in
all my goodwill may I let you leave. But
slowly, as my numbed senses regain life.
And my deceived soul bends forward and
cries, my limping self walks steps enough
to see how far you had left me behind.

You lifted me to a height, neared me till a point, embraced but a part of me. You spoke to me half the truth, told me just half the story. You revealed yourself to me only in part. I hang in uncertainty. I suffer in search of completion.

Why have you severed a part of you,
and named it me?

As water slips from sand, as the bird leaves the cliff. As spring abandons the forest, as the kiss leaves the lip, and the tear the eye, you left me. Your presence is felt, your fragrance smelt. Yet there is a void. Just as when air leaves the sky.

Either take me with you, or come with me. For life gains meaning only when you are with me. It seems our togetherness is just starting. When will the time come when there will be no parting?

If you open this cage and let this bird fly,
it will fly to you.

Sweet is the wait, sweeter the fulfillment.
One goes, one goes on.

You come in pair, that of a storm and a calm. At once, a wound and a balm.

For you what are months, years or lifetimes? With patience you wait for the birds to return to the nest. But for me, who can see nothing beyond now, to be without you today is indeed a great test!

When I ask of you a favor, it shall be one unimaginable by mortals. Or else what use is thy blessing! Why expect ordinary boons—extraordinary help must flow from a divine being such as you. My thirst is growing, master!

When will you emerge from your hiding, blessed one! When shall your chariot appear in sight? I look for you in the dust and the clouds, in the sweat of heat and showers of rain. Which is the rope I can pull that you return to me? How long is the wait left O friend? Life is shedding its joy. Colors of hope are fast fading. It is difficult to be without you now. Give a clue.

*Come—till there are bones remaining
in my frame that can run to welcome
thee. Till my eyes are hung in their
sockets to witness thee. I took birth to
love you, do not keep yourself away!
There is no more moment to waste.
I have not eternity, such as you.*

Let me see eyeful of you, this day shall not dawn again. Let me shed tearful of joy, this moment shall pass. Let me leap all over you, like flame over oil. Give your hand in mine, before you melt, and I perish.

Will my whole life get past me in this wait? When finally you arrive, so may also my end. Awaiting me as eagerly and as long as I awaited you. As you come from one door, I may have to leave through the next. Two bubbles that we are may never burst into one another. Is this our, rather my destiny?

I bet on thee, and lost all else.

I long to long for you. I have cherished you enough to know not to merge too soon, but stay on the verge of merging all the time.

73

As a ray of light snaking through dark terrain, I reflect on objects on my way through time. Illuminating them, but adding to me no shine. Lest I lose the way, worse, forget that I am thine, O my source, find me!

This heart, like Hanuman, expands to contain you, shrinks when you move away.

75

If distance will bring you closer, I shall stretch my wings wider than they can stretch, and fly far away.

*Strength to face you, courage to part,
penance to wait. Innate gifts or
practice of lifetimes?*

You can tempt me not with the sweetmeats of worldly splendor. I want the dispassion you revel in. You can sway me not with promise of fulfillment. I wish to empty myself in thy fullness.

*Just a glimpse of you, just a brush.
And you dispel all fear. How fascinating
a complete encounter with you will be,
master!*

Memories of your touch, difficult to bear.
Keep away, keep away, lest I tear.

When everything gets over,
why does nothing still remain?

Soul the fluttering bird. Flesh the cage.
Breath at guard. Moments of its rest,
hope for release.

*Now you will not be enough or
a mere being with you. I wish to
become you. Be you. I can no longer
bask in the shade of your glare. I
wish to become the strands of your
long hair. I wish no longer to follow
your print, rather become your
footprint. I am tired of calling ma,
ma—I wish to know Brahma!*

Lone bird sits on thorn. Single not thirsty.
Watchful, intent. At the ready.

Rid me of two. Let only one remain.
Just you.

UNION

Now that you are here,
don't I know you were always so.

I knew not my beginning, nor my end. Till I met you and followed your gaze. Then I knew, that in the depths of me that your eyes touch, I begin. And end.

How would I have realized that you are so close. How would I have known that you are so dear. Blessed are the pangs of pain. Welcome are the tears.

As the world slumbers, I awake,
sensing you nearer than breath.
Who are you to me, if not me.

Like a flower offered at the altar, an
incense that has been lit,
I await, what's next?

Today I know that every hap had a cause. Behind every curse was a tender blessing. Each storm brought with it a strange protection. And fierce love saw me through dangerous encounters. That the invisible hand has carried me all along, I know today.

*Move with me to where you are. Take me
to the ground on which you stand. It must
be cruel to have one like me follow! I halt
at too many places for rest and tea. Stop
too many a time to think if I still wish to
follow thee. But as you get up to leave,
I march right behind. Why do you
hasten? Aren't you already there
where you taketh me?*

What can I ever do for you, master?
I, who errs at every step. I, who fails every
test. I can only watch, as much as you
allow me to. I can love, as much as
I am destined. And praise you in words
that you lend to my lips.

Total renewal, fresh birth. No memory of yester nor thoughts of yonder. Delivered, yet in (nurturing) womb.

Everything is fearful. Everything is futile.
But if for you, life gains meaning.
Every action becomes a holy ritual.
Each moment turns divine.

Now you are watching me closely, the game has begun. Now you are spending each minute with me, the sharing has begun. Besides me there is only you. Not that you were not so before. But the veil has dropped only now, and I can sense your presence for sure. You love me more than I ever imagined to be. Are keener to bless me than I could ever see. I needlessly doubted and complained about the delay, when each day brought me closer to you like a relay. Now that so much is happening on which I have no say, I kneel in deep gratitude and obey!

Your presence, like elephant feet,
tramples upon the forest of my existence.
Nothing remains after you leave. Just cues
of what previously grew.

*With you O master, each minute a quest
is changed, a nest is shaken. A contract
thwarted, a chain is broken. With you,
O master, each second an hour is stolen.
You are leading me through a journey
that you tread once, are telling me that
the landscapes are as smelly as the
dumps. You shall lift me beyond both,
and turn me into a cloud. I know this
today beyond doubt.*

Now you may drop your impregnable
boundaries, for I have traveled
a distance too close.

*I realized this body of clay was indeed a
living temple, the day you stirred in mine.
I have found the center, the point. It was
always there, but in between had stood
the mind. You have been so kind—I now
revel in my own divinity. To offer
incense to you where is the time!*

*Stranded on street. Whiff of breeze plants
me in your lap, like never away.*

In the company of the beloved, all rules relax. All norms fail. Do the do's and don'ts before the curtain rises, and after it falls. But when the moon is full in sight, you are drunk without wine, stripped till your soul. Nothing is left of you that can be hidden. Nothing remains to be revealed.

Now that I have been lit, not even gods
know how bright or long I shall burn.

*My heart quivers to acknowledge that it
is thy bride. That thy feet are my lord.
The meeting of our eyes is the
culmination of our union.*

As the bell hung around cow's neck resounds with the slightest stir, so do I, so do I—as I sense you around me. As your presence rises and encircles, pain and bliss embrace each other in embracing me.

*Gone are the days I spent in yearning
to see you. With your grace, I now
rejoice in our silent communion.*

Deep stillness, relentless calm. Just ask for two tears, for pair of feet to smear.

*I salute you, for your lone quest
and our common victories.*

www.ingramcontent.com/pod-product-compliance
Lightning Source LLC
Chambersburg PA
CBHW020733160726
47993CB00006B/2439